DELICIC
DESSEKT
RECIPES

CUSTARDS AND
PUDDINGS

Niki Fletcher

Table of Contents

Crème Caramel Squares

Ingredients:

- 1½ cups graham cracker crumbs
- ☐ cup butter, melted
- 8 ounces cream cheese, softened
- ¼ cup sugar
- 3¼ cups cold milk, divided
- 8 ounces non-dairy whipped topping, divided
- 1 (3.4 ounce) package vanilla instant pudding
- 1 (3.4 ounce) package butterscotch instant pudding
- ☐ cup caramel ice cream topping

Procedure:

1. Mix the graham crumbs and butter and press the mixture onto the bottom of 9 x 13-inch dish.
2. Refrigerate the crust while preparing the filling.

3.   Beat the cream cheese, sugar and ¼ cup milk in a large bowl until blended.

4.   Fold in 1 cup of the whipped topping.

5.   Spread the mixture over the over crust.

6.   In a separate bowl for each flavor, beat the pudding mix with 1½ cups of the remaining milk for 2 minutes.

7.   Pour the pudding in layers over the cream cheese filling.

8.   Top with the remaining whipped topping.

9.   Refrigerate overnight.

10. Drizzle with the caramel topping just before serving.

Pineapple Pistachio Pudding

Ingredients:

- 1 (3.4 ounce) package pistachio instant pudding
- 1 (20 ounce) can crushed pineapple, undrained
- ½ cup chopped walnuts
- 4¼ cups miniature marshmallows, divided
- 16 ounces non-dairy whipped topping
- 3 maraschino cherries with stems

Procedure:

1. Stir the pudding mix, pineapple with juice, walnuts and 1 cup of the marshmallows in a large bowl until well blended.
2. Fold in 8 ounces of the whipped topping.

3. Put the remaining whipped topping into a separate medium bowl and fold in 2 cups of the marshmallows.

4. Put ½ of the pudding mixture into a large serving bowl.

5. Cover with a layer of ½ of the marshmallow mixture.

6. Repeat steps 4 and 5.

7. Top with the remaining 1¼ cups marshmallows and the cherries.

8. Refrigerate for at least 1 hour before serving.

Amaretto Pudding

Ingredients:

- 8 ounces Neufchatel cheese
- 2 cups milk, divided
- 1 (3.4 ounce) package vanilla flavor instant pudding
- 3 tablespoons almond liqueur
- 3 tablespoons grated semi-sweet chocolate, divided
- 8 ounces non-dairy whipped topping

Procedure:

1. Beat the Neufchatel and ½ cup of the milk in a medium bowl until they are well blended and smooth.
2. In a separate bowl, add the remaining 1½ cups milk to the pudding mix and beat for 2 minutes.
3. Add the pudding to the Neufchatel mixture and mix well.
4. Stir in the liqueur.
5. Pour the mixture into a serving bowl.
6. Sprinkle 2 tablespoons of the grated chocolate over the pudding mixture.
7. Top with the whipped topping.
8. Sprinkle with the remaining grated chocolate.
9. Refrigerate at least 1 hour before serving.

Pumpkin Maple Custard

Ingredients:

- 1 (5.4 ounce) package vanilla flavor cook and serve pudding
- 2 cups milk
- 1 cup canned pumpkin
- ½ teaspoon pumpkin pie spice
- 6 tablespoons maple syrup
- 6 ginger snap cookies
- ½ cup chopped pecans, toasted

Procedure:

1. Mix the pudding mix, milk, pumpkin and spice in large microwaveable bowl until they are well blended.
2. Microwave as directed on the package for cooking the pudding.
3. Cool for 5 minutes.
4. Put 1 tablespoon of the syrup into each of 6 custard cups and cover it with pudding.
5. Top the pudding with the ginger snaps.
6. Cover tightly and refrigerate for 4 hours.
7. Run a knife around the edge of each custard cup to loosen the dessert just before serving.
8. Invert the cups onto dessert plates and top with nuts.

Maple Walnut Tapioca Pudding

Ingredients:

- 1 egg
- 2½ cups milk
- ½ cup maple syrup
- 3 tablespoons instant tapioca
- 1 tablespoon firmly packed brown sugar
- ☐ cup chopped walnuts, toasted
- 1 teaspoon vanilla

Procedure:

1. Beat the egg, milk and syrup in large saucepan until they are well blended.
2. Add the tapioca and sugar and mix well.
3. Let the mixture stand for 5 minutes.
4. Bring the mixture to a full rolling boil on medium heat, stirring constantly.
5. Remove the pan from the heat.
6. Stir in the walnuts and vanilla.
7. Cool for 20 minutes.
8. Serve warm or chilled.
9. Stir before serving.

Apple Tapioca Pudding

Ingredients:

- 2 cups apple juice
- ☐ cup sugar
- 3 tablespoons instant tapioca

Procedure:

1. Mix all of the ingredients in a medium saucepan.
2. Let the mixture stand for 5 minutes.
3. Bring the mixture to a full rolling boil on medium heat, stirring constantly.
4. Remove the pan from the heat.
5. Cool the pudding for 20 minutes.
6. Stir the pudding.
7. Serve warm or chilled.

Eggnog Tapioca Pudding

Ingredients:

- ☐ cup sugar
- 3 tablespoons instant tapioca
- 3 cups milk
- 1 egg, well beaten
- ½ teaspoon rum extract
- ⅛ teaspoon ground nutmeg

Procedure:

1. Mix the sugar, tapioca, milk and egg in a medium saucepan.
2. Let the mixture stand for 5 minutes.
3. Cook on medium heat until the mixture comes to full boil, stirring constantly.
4. Remove the mixture from the heat.
5. Stir in the rum extract and nutmeg.
6. Cool the pudding for 20 minutes.
7. Stir the pudding.
8. Serve warm or chilled.

Pineapple Tapioca Pudding

Ingredients:

- 2½ cups pineapple-orange-banana juice blend
- ¼ cup instant tapioca
- 2 tablespoons butter
- 4 cups fresh pineapple chunks
- 1 tablespoon firmly packed light brown sugar
- ½ teaspoon ground nutmeg
- ¼ teaspoon salt
- 8 ounces non-dairy whipped topping
- 1 cup flaked coconut, toasted

Procedure:

1. Mix the juice and tapioca in a medium bowl.
2. Let the mixture stand for 5 minutes.
3. Melt the butter in a large saucepan on medium heat.
4. Add the pineapple, brown sugar, nutmeg and salt.
5. Cook the mixture for 5 minutes, stirring frequently.
6. Add the tapioca mixture and stir.
7. Bring the mixture to a full boil, stirring constantly.
8. Remove the pan from the heat.
9. Cool 20 minutes.
10. Transfer to a serving bowl.
11. Refrigerate overnight.
12. Top the pudding with the whipped topping and sprinkle with the coconut just before serving.

Dark Chocolate Tapioca Pudding

Ingredients:

- 1 egg
- ☐ cup sugar
- 3 tablespoons instant tapioca
- 3½ cups milk
- 2 squares unsweetened chocolate
- 1 teaspoon vanilla

Procedure:

1. Beat the egg lightly in a medium saucepan with a wire whisk.
2. Add the sugar and tapioca and mix well.
3. Gradually add the milk, beating well after each addition.
4. Let the mixture stand for 5 minutes.
5. Add the chocolate.
6. Bring the mixture to a boil on medium heat, stirring constantly.
7. Reduce heat to medium-low and cook until the chocolate is completely melted, stirring constantly.
8. Remove the pan from the heat.
9. Stir in the vanilla.
10. Cool for 20 minutes and stir.
11. Serve warm or chilled.

Fluffy Tapioca Cream Pudding

Ingredients:

- 1 egg, separated
- 6 tablespoons sugar, divided
- 3 tablespoon instant tapioca
- 2 cups milk
- 1 teaspoon vanilla

Procedure:

1. Beat the egg white until it is foamy.
2. Gradually add 3 tablespoons sugar, beating until soft peaks form.
3. Mix the tapioca, the remaining sugar, milk and egg yolk in medium saucepan.
4. Let the mixture stand for 5 minutes.
5. Cook on medium heat, stirring constantly, until the mixture comes to full boil.
6. Remove the pan from the heat.
7. Quickly stir the egg white mixture into the hot tapioca until it is well blended.
8. Stir in the vanilla.
9. Cool for 20 minutes and then stir.
10. Serve warm or chilled.

Fluffy Raspberry Tapioca Pudding

Ingredients:

- 1 egg
- 2¾ cups milk
- ☐ cup sugar
- 3 tablespoons instant tapioca
- 1 teaspoon vanilla
- 1 cup non-dairy whipped topping
- 2 tablespoons seedless raspberry jam

Procedure:

1. Beat the egg and milk in a saucepan until they are well blended.
2. Stir in the sugar and tapioca.
3. Let the mixture stand for 5 minutes.
4. Bring the mixture to a full rolling boil on medium heat, stirring constantly.
5. Remove the pan from the heat.
6. Stir in the vanilla.
7. Pour the pudding into a medium bowl and place plastic wrap directly on the surface of the pudding.
8. Refrigerate for 1 hour or until the pudding is cooled.
9. Gently stir in the whipped topping.
10. Add the jam and stir slightly to swirl.
11. Serve immediately.

Cookies and Cream Pudding

Ingredients:

- 8 chocolate sandwich cookies, divided
- 1 (3.4 ounce) package vanilla instant pudding
- 2 cups cold milk
- ¾ cup non-dairy whipped topping, divided

Procedure:

1. Break 1 cookie into 4 pieces and reserve for use as a garnish.
2. Crush the remaining cookies.
3. Beat the pudding mix and milk for 2 minutes.
4. Stir in the crushed cookies and ½ cup of the whipped topping.
5. Spoon into 4 dessert dishes.
6. Top each dish with ¼ of the remaining whipped topping and the reserved cookie pieces.
7. Refrigerate until ready to serve.

Vanilla Rice Pudding

Ingredients:

- 1 egg
- 4 cups milk
- 1 (3.4 ounce) package vanilla cook and serve pudding
- 1 cup instant white rice, uncooked
- ¼ cup raisins
- ¼ teaspoon ground cinnamon
- ⅛ teaspoon ground nutmeg

Procedure:

1. Beat the egg in large saucepan.
2. Gradually add the milk, beating until well blended.
3. Add the pudding mix and stir 2 minutes.
4. Stir in the rice and raisins.
5. Bring the mixture to a full rolling boil on medium heat, stirring constantly.
6. Remove the pan from the heat.
7. Cool for 5 minutes, stirring occasionally.
8. Pour into a 1½-quart serving bowl.
9. Sprinkle the cinnamon and nutmeg evenly over the top of the pudding.
10. Serve warm.

Pumpkin Mousse

Ingredients:

- 3 cups cold milk
- 2 (1.5 ounce) packages vanilla fat free sugar free instant pudding
- 1 (15 ounce) can pumpkin
- 1 teaspoon pumpkin pie spice
- 8 ounces non-dairy whipped topping, divided

Procedure:

1. Beat the milk and pudding mix for 2 minutes.
2. Blend in the pumpkin and the spice.
3. Fold in 1 cup of the whipped topping.
4. Pour into a serving bowl.
5. Refrigerate for1 hour.
6. Serve topped with the remaining whipped topping.

White Chocolate Mousse

Ingredients:

- 1 (6 square) package white chocolate
- 1½ cups heavy whipping cream, divided

Procedure:

1. Microwave the chocolate and ¼ cup cream in a large microwaveable bowl on high for 2 minutes or until the chocolate is almost melted, stirring after 1 minute.
2. Stir until the chocolate is completely melted.
3. Cool for 20 minutes or until the chocolate reaches room temperature, stirring occasionally.

4. Whip the remaining cream in a medium bowl until soft peaks form. (Do not over beat.)
5. Add ½ the whipped cream to the chocolate mixture.
6. Stir with a whisk until the mixture is well blended.
7. Stir in the remaining whipped cream.
8. Spoon into 6 dessert dishes.
9. Refrigerate for 2 hours

Autumn Harvest Rice Pudding

Ingredients:

- 3 cups milk, divided
- 1 cup instant white rice, uncooked
- 1 apple, chopped
- ☐ cup raisins
- ½ teaspoon ground cinnamon
- ¼ teaspoon ground nutmeg
- 1 (3.4 ounce) package vanilla instant pudding
- ¼ cup chopped walnuts

Procedure:

1. Bring 1 cup of the milk to boil in medium saucepan.
2. Stir in the rice, apple, raisins, cinnamon and nutmeg and cover.
3. Remove the pan from the heat and let stand 5 minutes.
4. Prepare the pudding with the remaining 2 cups milk in large bowl as directed on the package.
5. Add the rice mixture to the prepared pudding and mix well.
6. Stir in the walnuts.
7. Cover the surface of the pudding with plastic wrap and cool for at least 5 minutes.
8. Serve warm or chilled.

Rice Pudding with Figs and Grappa

Ingredients:

- Pinch of salt
- ½ cup uncooked rice
- 3 cups whole milk
- ¾ cup sugar
- ½ vanilla bean, split
- 2 large eggs
- 2 large egg yolks
- 1 cup mascarpone
- 6 dried figs
- ½ cup water
- ½ cup grappa or brandy
- 2 tablespoons sugar

Procedure:

1. Cook the rice in a saucepan of boiling water with the pinch of salt until the rice is almost tender.
2. Drain the rice and combine it with the milk, sugar, and split vanilla bean.
3. Bring the mixture to a boil, then reduce the heat and simmer uncovered, stirring frequently, until the rice is very tender.
4. Whisk together the eggs and the egg yolks.
5. Add ¼ cup of the rice to the egg mixture, stirring constantly.
6. Add another ¼ cup of the rice to the egg mixture, stirring constantly.
7. Add the egg mixture to the remaining rice and simmer, stirring frequently, until the pudding begins to thicken.
8. Remove the pan from the heat and stir in the mascarpone.
9. Remove the vanilla bean.
10. Spoon the pudding into 6 dessert dishes and cover the surface of each with plastic wrap.
11. Refrigerate the pudding for at least 3 hours.

12. Remove the stems from the figs.
13. Combine the figs, water, grappa and sugar in a pan and bring it to a boil.
14. Reduce the heat to medium and cook, stirring frequently for 20 minutes.
15. Cool the compote to room temperature and then quarter the figs.
16. Serve the fig compote on top of the pudding.

Cinnamon and Raisin Rice Pudding

Ingredients:

- 1□ cups water
- 1□ cups instant brown rice, uncooked
- ½ cup raisins
- ½ cup sour cream
- 1 tablespoon brown sugar
- ½ teaspoon ground cinnamon
- ½ cup sliced almonds

Procedure:

1. Bring the water to boil on medium-high heat.
2. Add the rice and raisins and stir.
3. Cover.
4. Reduce the heat to medium-low and simmer for 5 minutes.
5. Remove the pan from the heat and let stand, covered, for 5 minutes.
6. Mix the sour cream, brown sugar and cinnamon until well blended.
7. Add the sour cream mixture to the rice mixture and mix well.
8. Turn the pudding into a serving bowl and sprinkle with the almonds.
9. Serve either warm or chilled.

Warm Peanut Butter Pudding

Ingredients:

- 1 (3.9 ounce) package chocolate instant pudding
- 2 cups cold milk
- ¼ cup creamy peanut butter
- ¼ cup non-dairy whipped topping

Procedure:

1. Beat the pudding mix and the milk for 2 minutes.
2. Spoon the pudding into 4 microwaveable dessert dishes and top each bowl with ¼ of the peanut butter.
3. Microwave on high for 30 seconds or until the peanut butter begins to melt and pudding is heated throughout.
4. Top each bowl of pudding with whipped topping.

Coconut Caramel Rice Pudding

Ingredients:

- 6 cups milk
- 3 cups cooked long-grain white rice, cooled
- 1 (14 ounce) bag caramels
- ½ cup flaked coconut

Procedure:

1. Unwrap all of the caramels.

2. Bring the milk to a boil in a large saucepan, and then reduce the heat to medium-low.

3. Gradually stir in the rice.

4. Add the caramels, a few at a time, while stirring.

5. Cook and stir the mixture until the caramels are completely melted and the pudding is thickened.

6. Stir in the coconut.

7. Pour the pudding into a serving bowl.

8. Refrigerate for at least 3 hours before serving.

Creamy Coconut Rice Pudding

Ingredients:

- 1 cup water
- ½ cup white rice, uncooked
- 2 cups milk
- ¼ cup sugar
- 1 teaspoon vanilla
- 4 ounces cream cheese, cubed
- ½ cup flake coconut, toasted
- ½ cup non-dairy whipped topping

Procedure:

1. Bring the water and rice to a boil on medium-high heat.
2. Cover and simmer on low heat for 8 to 10 minutes or until the water is absorbed.
3. Add the milk, sugar and vanilla and stir well.
4. Bring the mixture to a boil.
5. Cover and cook, stirring occasionally, on low heat for 20 to 25 minutes or until the pudding is thickened.
6. Reserve 1 tablespoon of the coconut for a garnish.
7. Remove the pudding from the heat and stir in the cream cheese and remaining coconut until the mixture is well blended.
8. Pour the pudding into a large serving bowl and cool slightly.
9. Refrigerate for at least 2 hours.
10. Top each serving with whipped topping and some of the reserved coconut.

Hawaiian Coconut Pudding

Ingredients:

- 2 cups coconut milk
- 1 cup milk
- 6 tablespoons sugar
- 5 tablespoons cornstarch
- ¼ teaspoon vanilla
- ¼ cup flaked coconut, toasted

Procedure:

1. Pour 1 cup of the coconut milk into a saucepan.
2. Combine the sugar and cornstarch and stir it into the coconut milk in the pan.
3. Add the vanilla.
4. Heat over low heat, stirring constantly, until the mixture is thickened.
5. Add the remaining coconut milk and milk.
6. Continue to heat, stirring constantly, until the pudding is thickened.
7. Pour into an 8-inch square pan.
8. Refrigerate overnight
9. Top with the flaked coconut prior to serving.

No-Bake Coconut Flan

Ingredients:

- 1 (8-serving size) package instant flan custard with caramel sauce
- 2½ cups milk
- 1 (15 ounce) can cream of coconut
- 1 cup flaked coconut

Procedure:

1. Pour the caramel sauce into a 9 x 5-inch loaf pan and set aside.
2. Combine the milk, cream of coconut and coconut in a large saucepan and stir in the flan mix.
3. Bring the mixture to a full rolling boil on medium heat, stirring constantly.
4. Remove the pan from the heat.
5. Carefully the pour custard mixture over the caramel layer in the loaf pan.
6. Refrigerate for 2 hours or until the custard is set.
7. Unmold the flan by running a small knife or metal spatula around the edge of the pan.
8. Invert the flan onto plate and shake gently to loosen.
9. Serve immediately.

Coffee Panna Cotta

Ingredients:

- 32 ounces plain yogurt
- 2 envelopes unflavored gelatin
- 2 tablespoons instant coffee
- ¾ cup sugar
- ¼ teaspoon almond extract
- ½ cup non-dairy whipped topping
- 2 tablespoons chopped almonds

Procedure:

1. Mix the yogurt, gelatin, coffee granules and sugar in a medium microwaveable bowl.
2. Microwave on high for 2½ minutes or until the gelatin is completely dissolved, stirring after 1½ minutes.
3. Stir in the almond extract.
4. Pour into a 9-inch pie plate that has been sprayed with cooking spray.
5. Refrigerate for 3 hours or until the pudding is set.
6. Unmold the dessert onto a serving plate.
7. Top with the whipped topping and almonds just before serving.

Mocha Pudding

Ingredients:

- 1 (3.9 ounce) package chocolate instant pudding
- 1½ cups cold milk
- ½ cup strong coffee, cooled
- 12 chocolate sandwich cookies, divided
- 1½ cups non-dairy whipped topping

Procedure:

1. Beat the pudding mix, milk and coffee in medium bowl for 2 minutes.
2. Put half the pudding into 4 dessert glasses.
3. Top each with 2 crumbled cookies.
4. Fold the whipped topping into the remaining pudding.
5. Spoon over the crushed cookies.
6. Top with each dish with one of the remaining whole cookies.

Banana Split Pudding

Ingredients:

- 1 (3.4 ounce) package French vanilla instant pudding
- 1 cup cold milk
- 8 ounces non-dairy whipped topping, divided
- 24 chocolate wafers, divided
- 2 small bananas
- 8 teaspoons pineapple ice cream topping
- 8 maraschino cherries
- ¼ cup chopped nuts

Procedure:

1. Beat the pudding mix and milk in large bowl for 2 minutes.
2. Stir in 1½ cups of the whipped topping
3. Spread into an 8-inch square pan.

56

4. Freeze for 3 hours or until the pudding is firm enough to scoop.

5. Crush 16 of the chocolate wafers.

6. Spoon 1 tablespoon of the crushed wafers into each of 8 parfait glasses or dessert dishes.

7. Scoop ¼ cup of the pudding mixture into each glass.

8. Sprinkle with the remaining crushed wafers.

9. Cut the bananas into quarters by cutting each in half lengthwise and then cut each piece in half crosswise.

10. Stand 1 banana piece in each parfait glass.

11. Put 1 teaspoon pineapple ice cream topping into each glass.

12. Fill the glass with the remaining whipped topping and the whole wafers.

13. Sprinkle chopped nuts on top of each glass.

14. Top each glass with one of the cherries.

15. Serve immediately.

Cream Cheese Banana Pudding

Ingredients:

- 8 ounces cream cheese
- 1 (14 ounce) can sweetened condensed milk
- 1 (8 serving size) package instant vanilla pudding mix
- 3 cups cold milk
- 1 teaspoon vanilla extract
- 8 ounces non-dairy whipped topping
- 4 bananas, sliced
- ½ (12 ounce) package vanilla wafers

Procedure:

1. In a large bowl, beat the cream cheese until it is fluffy.
2. Beat in the condensed milk, pudding mix, cold milk and vanilla until the mixture is smooth.
3. Fold in ½ of the whipped topping.
4. Line the bottom of a 9 x 13 inch dish with the vanilla wafers.
5. Arrange the sliced bananas evenly over the wafers.
6. Spread the pudding mixture on top of the bananas.
7. Top with the remaining whipped topping.
8. Refrigerate overnight.

Quick Banana Pudding

Ingredients:

- 2 (1.4 ounce) packages vanilla sugar free instant pudding
- 4 cups milk
- 47 vanilla wafers, divided
- 5 to 6 medium ripe bananas, sliced (about 3 cups), divided
- 8 ounces non-dairy whipped topping

Procedure:

1. Prepare the pudding with the milk as directed on the package.
2. Put ½ cup of the pudding in the bottom of 2-quart serving bowl.
3. Top the pudding with 8 vanilla wafers.
4. Add a layer of sliced bananas.
5. Top the bananas with 1 cup of the pudding.
6. Stand 12 wafers around the outside edge of the serving bowl.
7. Top the pudding layer with 12 vanilla wafers.
8. Add a layer of sliced bananas
9. Top the bananas with 1 cup of the pudding.
10. Top the pudding with 15 vanilla wafers.
11. Add a layer of the remaining sliced bananas.
12. Top the bananas with the remaining pudding.
13. Refrigerate overnight to soften the vanilla wafers.
14. To serve, spread the whipped topping over the pudding.

Easy Banana Crème

Ingredients:

- 1 (3.4 ounce) package banana instant pudding
- 2 cups milk
- 1 cup bananas, diced
- 1 cup miniature marshmallows
- 2 tablespoons maraschino cherries, chopped

Procedure:

1. Combine the milk and pudding mixture and beat the mixture for 2 minutes.
2. Stir in the bananas and marshmallows.
3. Divide the mixture between 4 dessert cups.
4. Top with the diced cherries.
5. Refrigerate for at least 1 hour.

Banana Cream Pudding

Ingredients:

- ☐ cup brown sugar
- 2 bananas, sliced
- 1 slice white bread
- 2 eggs, beaten
- ½ cup milk
- ¼ teaspoon vanilla extract

Procedure:

1. Cut the bread into 9 equal squares.
2. Place the bananas and bread in the top of a double boiler.
3. Combine the eggs, milk, sugar and pour over the banana mixture.
4. Cover tightly and cook over boiling water for 35 minutes.
5. Serve warm.

Creamy Banana Pudding

Ingredients:

- 1 (14 ounce) can sweetened condensed milk
- 1½ cups cold water
- 1 (3.4 ounce) package instant vanilla pudding mix
- 2 cups heavy whipping cream
- 36 vanilla wafers
- 3 medium bananas, sliced and dipped in lemon juice

Procedure:

1. In a large bowl, combine the sweetened condensed milk and water.
2. Add pudding mix and beat until the mixture is well blended.
3. Chill for 5 minutes.
4. Whip the cream until stiff peaks form.
5. Fold the whipped cream into the pudding mixture.
6. Spoon 1 cup of the pudding mixture into a 2½-quart glass serving bowl.
7. Top with □ of the vanilla wafers.
8. Top the wafers with □ of the bananas.
9. Top the bananas with □ of the remaining pudding.
10. Repeat steps 7-9 twice.
11. Refrigerate overnight.

Mango Pudding

Ingredients:

- 2 medium ripe mangos
- 1 envelope unflavored gelatin
- ½ cup water
- ☐ cup white sugar
- 1 cup coconut milk

Procedure:

1. Scoop out the fruit of the mango and place it in a blender.
2. Purée the mango until it is smooth.
3. Leave the mango in the blender.

4. In a saucepan, combine the water and the gelatin and allow the gelatin to soften for 5 minutes.

5. Bring the water to a boil while stirring constantly to dissolve the gelatin.

6. Remove the gelatin from the heat.

7. Add the sugar to the gelatin mixture and stir until it is dissolved.

8. Add the gelatin mixture and the coconut milk to the mango in the blender.

9. Pulse briefly until all the ingredients are combined.

10. Pour the pudding into dessert bowls and refrigerate for at least 2 hours.

Mango Lime Pudding

Ingredients:

- 2 envelopes unflavored gelatin
- ½ cup water
- 4 to 6 ripe mangos, peeled and diced, or 5 cups diced frozen mango, thawed
- 1 (14 ounce can) sweetened condensed milk
- 4 tablespoons lime juice

Procedure:

1. Sprinkle the gelatin over the water in a small bowl and let it stand until softened, about 5 minutes.

2. Microwave on high, uncovered, until the gelatin has completely dissolved but the liquid is not boiling—10 to 20 seconds.

3. Stir until the gelatin is completely dissolved.

4. Place the diced mango in a blender and purée until it is smooth. You should have 2 cups of purée.

5. Mix the mango purée, sweetened condensed milk and lime juice in a medium bowl.

6. Slowly stir in the softened gelatin mixture until the mixture is well combined.

7. Lightly coat eight 6- to 10-ounce ramekins with cooking spray.

8. Divide the pudding among the ramekins.

9. Refrigerate for at least 2 hours.

Papaya Pudding

Ingredients:

- 1¼ cup milk
- ☐ cup semolina
- 1 envelope unflavored gelatin
- ☐ cup powdered sugar
- Juice and grated rind of 1 lemon
- Juice and grated rind of 1 orange
- 1 cup papaya pulp
- ☐ cup heavy whipping cream
- 1 fresh papaya

Procedure:

1. Put the milk in a saucepan and bring it to a boil.
2. Reduce the heat.
3. Stir in the semolina and simmer for 5 minutes.

4. Mix the gelatin and sugar together and then stir the mixture into the milk and semolina mixture until it dissolves.

5. Add the grated rind and the juices.

6. Stir in the mashed papaya pulp and cool.

7. Whip the cream until stiff peaks form and fold it into the mixture.

8. Pour the mixture into 9-inch ring mold that has been sprayed with cooking spray.

9. Refrigerate overnight.

10. Turn the pudding out onto a flat dish.

11. Scoop out the fresh papaya with a melon baller and pile the papaya balls in the center of the molded pudding.

Chai Latte Pudding

Ingredients:

- 2 cups cold milk
- 1 (3.4 ounce) package vanilla instant pudding
- ¼ cup café chai latte mix
- ½ cup non-dairy whipped topping
- ⅛ teaspoon ground cinnamon

Procedure:

1. Mix the pudding mix, tea mix and milk in a bowl and beat for 2 minutes.
2. Transfer the pudding mixture into a glass serving bowl or into individual dessert bowls.
3. Refrigerate the pudding for at least 1 hour.
4. Top with the whipped topping just before serving.
5. Sprinkle with the cinnamon.

Flan de Café con Leche

Ingredients:

- 4 tablespoons cornstarch
- 3 cups milk
- 1 cup heavy cream
- 2½ tablespoons instant coffee
- 1 cup sugar
- 2 eggs
- 8 ounces non-dairy whipped topping

Procedure:

1. In a bowl, whisk the cornstarch into the milk until it is smooth.

2. Place the milk mixture, heavy cream, instant coffee, and sugar into the top of a double boiler.

3. Stir the ingredients over medium heat until it is thick.

4. Cover and simmer for 10 minutes.

5. In a bowl, beat the eggs until they are frothy.

6. Take 1 cup of the milk mixture from the double boiler and slowly add it to the eggs, beating continuously.

7. Pour the egg mixture into the double boiler and beat the mixture until it is well mixed.

8. Cover and simmer for 2 minutes.

9. Remove the pudding from the heat and pour it into individual dessert cups.

10. Refrigerate overnight.

Cappuccino Pudding

Ingredients:

- 1 (1.5 ounce) package vanilla sugar free instant pudding
- 2 teaspoons instant coffee
- 2 cups cold milk
- ⅛ teaspoon ground cinnamon
- 1 cup non-dairy whipped topping

Procedure:

1. Beat the pudding mix, coffee granules and milk for 2 minutes.
2. Pour the mixture into 5 dessert dishes.
3. Refrigerate the pudding for 1 hour.
4. Mix the cinnamon into the whipped topping and spoon the mixture over the pudding.

Pudding Café

Ingredients:

- 2 cups cold milk
- 1 (3.4 ounce) package vanilla instant pudding mix
- ¼ cup French vanilla café
- 1 cup non-dairy whipped topping

Procedure:

1. Mix the milk, pudding mix and flavored instant coffee in a bowl.
2. Beat the mixture until it is until well blended.
3. Pour the mixture into a serving bowl and cover.
4. Refrigerate for at least 1 hour.
5. Top the pudding with the whipped topping just before serving.

Boiled Custard

Ingredients:

- 4 cups milk
- 4 whole eggs or 6 yolks
- 1 cup sugar
- 2 teaspoons vanilla

Procedure:

1. Put the milk in double boiler and heat it to the boiling point.
2. Beat the eggs and the sugar until they are frothy.
3. Add the egg mixture to the milk and cook, stirring constantly, until the custard coats the spoon.
4. Remove the custard from the heat and mix in the vanilla.
5. Refrigerate until cold.

Chocolate Raspberry Pudding

Ingredients:

- 1½ cups boiling water
- 1 (0.3 ounce) package raspberry sugar free gelatin
- ½ square bittersweet chocolate
- ½ cup miniature marshmallows
- ¾ cup non-dairy whipped topping
- ¼ cup fresh raspberries

Procedure:

1. Add the boiling water to the gelatin mix and stir until the gelation is completely dissolved and then set aside.
2. Place the chocolate, marshmallows and the whipped topping in a medium microwaveable bowl.
3. Microwave on high power for 1 minute or until the marshmallows are completely melted and mixture is well blended when stirred.
4. Gradually add the gelatin to the chocolate mixture, beating with a whisk after each addition until the mixture is well blended.
5. Pour the pudding into 4 dessert dishes.
6. Refrigerate for 4 hours or until the pudding is firm.
7. Top with the berries just before serving.

Cinnamon Chocolate Pudding

Ingredients:

- 1 (1.4 oz.) package chocolate sugar free instant pudding
- ½ teaspoon ground cinnamon
- 2 cups milk
- ½ cup non-dairy whipped topping

Procedure:

1. Beat the pudding mix, cinnamon and milk for 2 minutes.
2. Stir in the whipped topping.
3. Pour into a serving bowl or individual pudding cups.
4. Refrigerate the pudding until it is ready to serve.

Quick Chocolate Marshmallow Pudding

Ingredients:

- 1 (3.9 ounce) package chocolate instant pudding
- 1 cup miniature marshmallows
- ☐ cup non-dairy whipped topping

Procedure:

1. Prepare the pudding as directed on package.
2. Stir in the marshmallows.
3. Spoon evenly into 5 microwaveable dessert dishes.
4. Microwave on high for 30 seconds or until the marshmallows begin to melt and the pudding is heated throughout.
5. Top each serving with 2 tablespoons of the whipped topping.

Chocolate Marshmallow Pudding

Ingredients:

- ☐ cup sugar
- ☐ cup flour
- ⅛ teaspoon salt
- 3 teaspoons cocoa
- 2¼ cup milk
- 1 egg, beaten
- ½ teaspoon vanilla
- ½ cup marshmallows

Procedure:

1. Mix the sugar, flour, salt and cocoa in double boiler.
2. Slowly add the milk and cook until the mixture is thick enough to coat the back of the spoon.
3. Add the egg and cook an additional 2 minutes.
4. Remove the pudding from the heat.
5. Add the vanilla and marshmallows and beat for 3 minutes.
6. Refrigerate until cold.

Easy Chocolate Mousse

Ingredients:

- 1 cup semisweet chocolate chips
- 1 egg, room temperature
- 1 teaspoon vanilla extract
- 1 cup heavy cream
- 8 ounces non-dairy whipped topping
- Chocolate curls or cocoa, for garnish

Procedure:

1. Place the chocolate chips, egg and vanilla in a blender and chop the chocolate chips into flakes.

2. Heat the cream until it is very hot and small bubbles appear at the edge, but do not boil.

3. With the blender running, pour in the hot cream.

4. Blend until the chocolate is melted and the mixture is smooth.

5. Pour the pudding into dessert dishes, cover with plastic wrap, and chill until the pudding is firm.

6. Serve topped with whipped topping and chocolate curls or cocoa powder.

Rocky Road Pudding

Ingredients:

- 2 cups cold milk
- 2 (3.9 ounce) packages chocolate instant pudding
- 2 cups non-dairy whipped topping
- 1 cup cocktail peanuts
- 4 squares semi-sweet chocolate, chopped
- 1 cup miniature marshmallows

Procedure:

1. Mix the pudding and the milk in a large bowl and beat for 2 minutes.
2. Fold in the whipped topping.
3. Add the remaining ingredients and stir gently until the mixture is well blended.
4. Pour into a large glass serving bowl or 12 individual serving bowls.
5. Refrigerate at least 1 hour before serving.

Marshmallow Pudding

Ingredients:

- 1 (14 ounce) can sweetened condensed milk
- 30 large marshmallows
- 1 (15 ounce) can crushed pineapple, drained
- 1 cup heavy whipping cream
- ½ cup chopped nuts
- ¼ cup maraschino cherries, chopped

Procedure:

1. In a double boiler, combine the marshmallows and the condensed milk and stir over hot water until the marshmallows are melted.
2. Fold in the pineapple.
3. Remove the mixture from the heat.
4. Whip the cream until stiff peaks form.
5. Fold the whipped cream into the pudding mixture.
6. Add the nuts and cherries and stir well.
7. Refrigerate until cold.

Lime Pudding

Ingredients:

- 2 large limes
- 1 (14 ounce) can sweetened condensed milk
- 1 cup heavy whipping cream

Procedure:

1. Grate the peel from 1 lime and squeeze the juice from both limes.
2. In large bowl, mix the lime juice, condensed milk, and lime peel until the mixture is thickened.
3. Whip the cream until stiff peaks form.
4. Fold the whipped cream into the lime mixture.
5. Refrigerate at least 2 hours.

Mint Chocolate Chip Pudding

Ingredients:

- 1 (3.4 ounce) package vanilla pudding mix
- 2 cups milk
- 4-5 drops peppermint extract
- 4 drops green food coloring
- ½ cup miniature chocolate chips

Procedure:

1. Mix the pudding with the milk in a medium bowl.
2. Whisk for at least two minutes.
3. Add the peppermint extract and food coloring and stir until the pudding is a uniform green color.
4. Put the pudding in the refrigerator for 5 minutes
5. Stir in the chocolate chips.

Chocolate Yogurt Pudding

Ingredients:

- 1 cup sugar
- ¼ cup unsweetened cocoa powder
- 1 envelope unflavored gelatin
- 1 (12 ounce) can evaporated milk
- 16 ounces vanilla yogurt
- 1 teaspoon vanilla
- 2 medium bananas, sliced

Procedure:

1. In a medium saucepan combine the sugar, cocoa powder, and gelatin.
2. Gradually stir in the evaporated milk.
3. Cook and stir over medium heat until the mixture comes to a boil and the gelatin is dissolved.
4. Remove the pan from the heat and cool slightly.
5. Stir the yogurt and vanilla into the chocolate mixture.
6. Divide the banana slices among 8 dessert dishes.
7. Spoon the chocolate pudding over the banana slices.
8. Refrigerate overnight.

Peanut Putter Pudding

Ingredients:

- ☐ cup sugar
- 4½ teaspoons cornstarch
- ¼ teaspoon salt
- 1½ cups milk
- ½ cup half-and-half cream
- ½ cup creamy peanut butter
- 1 teaspoon vanilla extract

Procedure:

1. In a saucepan, combine the sugar, cornstarch and salt.
2. Gradually stir in the milk and cream.
3. Bring the mixture to a boil over medium heat, stirring constantly.
4. Cook and stir for an additional 2 minutes.
5. Remove the pan from the heat and stir in the peanut butter and vanilla until smooth.
6. Pour the pudding into a serving bowl.
7. Refrigerate overnight.

Butterscotch Pudding

Ingredients:

- 2¼ cups milk
- 1 cup heavy cream
- 6 tablespoons unsalted butter
- 1¼ cups light brown sugar, packed
- 3 egg yolks
- ¼ cup cornstarch
- ¼ teaspoon salt
- 1½ teaspoons pure vanilla extract

Procedure:

1. In a large saucepan, combine the milk and cream and bring the mixture to a simmer over medium heat.
2. Immediately turn off the heat and set aside.

3. In a large, heavy skillet, melt the butter over medium-high heat.

4. Stir in the brown sugar, raise the heat to medium-high, and cook 5 to 7 minutes, stirring constantly, to caramelize the mixture.

5. Stirring constantly, gradually add the brown sugar mixture to the milk mixture.

6. Put the egg yolks in a medium bowl and whisk in about ½ cup of the hot milk mixture.

7. Stir in the cornstarch and salt until they are dissolved.

8. Stir the cornstarch mixture back into the hot milk mixture in the saucepan.

9. Stirring constantly, cook over medium-high heat until the mixture is thick and just boiling.

10. Turn off the heat and stir in the vanilla extract.

11. Pour into a serving dish.

12. Refrigerate overnight.

Spiked Butterscotch Pudding

Ingredients:

- 3 tablespoons unsalted butter
- ½ cup plus 2 tablespoons packed brown sugar
- ⅛ teaspoon salt
- 3 tablespoons cornstarch
- 2 cups half-and-half
- 1 ½ tablespoons Scotch whiskey

Procedure:

1. Combine the butter, brown sugar and salt in a saucepan and cook over low heat, stirring constantly, until the butter is melted and the sugar is dissolved.

2. Stir the cornstarch into ½ cup of the half-and-half until the cornstarch is completely dissolved.

3. Add ½ cup of the half-and-half to the butter and sugar mixture and stir well.

4. Add the remaining half-and-half and the cornstarch mixture and stir well.

5. Turn up the heat to medium-high and cook the mixture, stirring constantly, until the mixture is thickened.

6. Remove the mixture from the heat and stir in the whiskey.

7. Spoon the pudding into 4 dessert dishes and cover the surface with plastic wrap.

8. Refrigerate at least 3 hours.

Irish Cream Chocolate Mousse

Ingredients:

- 1 (3.9 ounce) package chocolate instant pudding mix
- 1¼ cups cold milk
- ¼ cup Irish cream liqueur
- 8 ounces non-dairy whipped topping, divided
- ½ cup fresh raspberries

Procedure:

1. Beat the pudding mix, milk and liqueur in medium bowl for 2 minutes.
2. Stir in 1½ cups of the whipped topping.
3. Divide the pudding into dessert dishes.
4. Refrigerate for at least 20 minutes.
5. Top the pudding with the raspberries and the remaining whipped topping before serving.

Danish Rum Pudding with Raspberry Sauce

Ingredients:

- 1 tablespoon unflavored gelatin
- ¼ cup water
- 2 cups eggnog
- ☐ cup sugar
- 2 tablespoons cornstarch, divided
- 1 teaspoon rum extract
- 1 cup heavy whipping cream
- 1 (10 ounce) package frozen raspberries
- ½ cup currant jelly
- 1 tablespoon butter
- ¾ cup orange juice

Procedure:

1. Soften the gelatin in the water for 5 minutes.
2. Heat the eggnog in a saucepan.
3. Mix the sugar and 1 tablespoon of the cornstarch and add it to the eggnog.
4. Cook, stirring constantly, until the mixture is thickened.
5. Remove the pan from the heat and stir in the gelatin until it is dissolved.
6. Cool to room temperature and then beat in the rum extract.
7. Whip the cream until stiff peaks form.
8. Fold the whipped cream into the eggnog pudding.
9. Divide the pudding into 6 dessert glasses and refrigerate overnight.
10. Thaw the raspberries.
11. Mix ¾ cup of the raspberries with the currant jelly in a saucepan and bring the mixture to a boil.
12. Reduce the heat.
13. Mix the remaining cornstarch and raspberries.
14. Add the mixture to the hot raspberries.

15. Cook, stirring constantly, until the mixture is thickened.
16. Remove the pan from the heat and allow the mixture to cool slightly.
17. Add the butter and stir until it is melted.
18. When the mixture reaches room temperature, stir in the orange juice and chill.
19. Top the pudding with the sauce.

Bourbon Custard

Ingredients:

- 6 large egg yolks
- ¼ cup sugar
- 1 teaspoon all-purpose flour
- Pinch salt
- 2 cups milk, warmed
- 1 tablespoon bourbon

Procedure:

1. Place a medium glass bowl in the refrigerator to chill.
2. Combine the egg yolks, sugar, flour, and salt in a nonreactive saucepan.
3. Beat until the mixture is a pale yellow.
4. Place the mixture over low heat and slowly stir in the warm milk.
5. Cook, stirring constantly, until the custard coats a wooden spoon quite thickly.
6. Immediately pour the custard into the chilled mixing bowl.
7. Cover and place the custard in the refrigerator for at least 2 hours.
8. Stir in the bourbon.

Banana Rum Custard

Ingredients:

- 4 egg yolks
- 2 cups half-and-half
- ¼ cup sugar
- ¼ teaspoon salt
- 1 tablespoon dark rum
- 1 teaspoon vanilla
- 6 medium bananas, thinly sliced

Procedure:

1. In the top of a double boiler over hot water, beat together the egg yolks, half-and-half, sugar and salt.

2. Continue cooking and stirring until the mixture is thick enough to coat a spoon.

3. Strain the custard.

4. Add the rum and vanilla and stir well.

5. Let cool to room temperature and then, cover, and chill.

6. When ready to serve, ladle the custard over thinly sliced bananas in parfait glasses.

Kumquat Pudding

Ingredients:

- 8 ounces cream cheese
- 5 ounces sour cream
- 2 cups kumquats, puréed
- ¾ cup sugar
- 8 ounces non-dairy whipped topping

Procedure:

1. Beat the cream cheese and sour cream until they are fluffy.
2. Mix in the kumquat purée and the sugar.
3. Fold in the whipped topping.
4. Refrigerate for at least two hours.

Vanilla Pudding

Ingredients:

- 3 cups milk, divided
- ¼ cup cornstarch
- ½ cup sugar
- ¼ teaspoon salt
- 1½ teaspoons vanilla extract

Procedure:

1. Scald 2□ cups of the milk.
2. Mix the cornstarch, sugar and salt and stir in the remaining □ cup milk.
3. Add the mixture to the scalded milk and cook over low heat, stirring constantly, until it is thickened and smooth.
4. Continue cooking for an additional 5 minutes.
5. Cool the pudding slightly and stir in the vanilla.
6. Pour into 6 serving dishes.
7. Refrigerate until ready to serve.

Chocolate Crumb Pudding

Ingredients:

- 4 eggs, separated
- 1 ounce sweet chocolate
- ¼ cup butter
- ½ cup milk
- ½ cup sugar
- 2 cups soft bread crumbs
- 1 cup blanched, slivered almonds
- 8 ounces non-dairy whipped topping (optional)

Procedure:

1. Beat the egg yolks in a small bowl.

2. In another bowl, beat the egg whites until stiff peaks form.

3. In top of a double boiler, heat the chocolate, butter, and milk.

4. Slowly add the beaten egg yolks and the sugar.

5. Cook, stirring occasionally, until the mixture is thickened.

6. Stir in the bread crumbs and almonds.

7. Fold in the beaten egg whites.

8. Cover and cook in a double boiler over simmering water for 25 minutes.

9. Serve either hot or cold and garnish with whipped topping if desired.

Strawberry Bread Pudding

Ingredients:

- 2 pints fresh strawberries
- 1 cup sugar
- ¼ teaspoon cinnamon
- Dash of ground cloves
- 2 tablespoons water
- 12 slices day-old bread
- ☐ cup melted butter
- 8 ounces non-dairy whipped topping

Procedure:

1. Reserve several strawberries for a garnish.
2. Cut the remaining strawberries in half and place them in a saucepan.
3. Add the sugar, cinnamon, cloves, and water to the saucepan and bring the mixture to a boil, stirring constantly.
4. Reduce the heat and simmer for 4 minutes.
5. Remove the crusts from the bread and butter both sides of each slice.
6. Line the bottom and sides of a 1½ quart baking dish and brush the edges of the bread with juice from the strawberry mixture.
7. Add alternate layers of strawberry mixture and bread.
8. Refrigerate overnight.
9. Top the pudding with the whipped topping and the reserved strawberries.

Classic Boiled Custard

Ingredients:

- ¾ cup sugar
- Pinch of salt
- 2½ tablespoons all-purpose flour
- 2 cups milk
- 4 eggs, separated
- 1 teaspoon vanilla

Procedure:

1. Beat the egg whites until stiff peaks form and set aside.
2. Combine the sugar, salt, and flour in a saucepan and slowly add the milk, stirring constantly.
3. Beat the egg yolks and stir them into the mixture.
4. Cook, stirring constantly, until the mixture is slightly thickened and coats the back of the spoon.
5. Remove the pan from the heat.
6. Beat the pudding mixture into the egg whites.
7. Stir in the vanilla.
8. Refrigerate overnight.

THANK YOU

Thank you for choosing *Delicious Dessert Recipes: Custards And Puddings* for improving your cooking skills! I hope you enjoyed the recipes while making them and tasting them! If you're interested in learning new recipes and new meals to cook, go and check out the other books of the serie.

CPSIA information can be obtained
at www.ICGtesting.com
Printed in the USA
BVHW061254140421
604894BV00013B/1496